Phillip Tilley

The Bartender's
JOKE
Book

WORKBOOK PRESS LLC
187 E Warm Springs Rd,
Suite B285, Las Vegas, NV 89119, USA

Website: https://workbookpress.com/
Hotline: 1-888-818-4856
Email: admin@workbookpress.com

Ordering Information:
Quantity sales. Special discounts are available on quantity purchases by corporations, associations, and others. For details, contact the publisher at the address above.

Library of Congress Control Number:
ISBN-13: 000-0-00000-000-0 (Paperback Version)
          000-0-00000-000-0 (Digital Version)

REV. DATE: 07/22/2022

THE BARTENDER'S JOKE BOOK

BY: PHILLIP TILLEY

DEDICATION

This book is dedicated to my son, Jeremy, who attended bartending school and learned that if a bartender has a good joke, they often get better tips.

1. Why should you never have sex with a prostitute that wears fishnet stockings?

You could get a case of crabs.

2. Why did the invisible man break up with his girlfriend?

They just stopped seeing each other!

3. Did you hear about the new drink in Montana called a Cowboy Cocktail?

It is a shot of vodka with a Viagra for a double stiff drink.

4. What pet name did the invisible man call his penis?

Mr. Hyde.

5. Why did the shop refuse to work on transmissions during the day?

They left transmission work for the 2nd shift.

6. Why did the guy have a smile face tattooed on his balls?

So, he would never have a sad sack.

7. Why did the porn star insist his jury consist only of other porn stars?

Not only would it be a jury of his peers, it would be a hung jury!

8. Why didn't Robin Hood need Viagra?

He was from Sherwood!

9. Where does a heroin addict keep his drugs?

In a junk drawer!

10. Why did the school teacher only have sex with virgins?

They were taut!

11. What's the best name for a porn starlet?

Phyllis up!

12. When I asked the female porn director if she was still looking for actors, what did she say?

Of course, I still have three openings!

13. What do Cops and Plastic Surgeons have in common?

They both like to make a good bust!

14. What happens if you eat marijuana brownies?

You become a weed-eater!

15. What happened when the porn star broke his penis during filming?

The Director has to recast his staff!

16. What does an attorney nick-named iron bottom do?

Files his briefs!

17. Why is a sleep number bed better than Viagra?

You can adjust the firmness!

18. Have you heard about the new alternative to Viagra called sound stage?

It lets you adjust the volume!

19. What do you call a nurse that has sex with her patients?

A sick fucker!

20. What do you call a married woman who has sex with a priest?

Hoy unfaithful!

21. How are prostitutes similar to the common cold?

They spread quickly!

22. What happened when the 400-pound man was buried?

The plot thickened!

23. What happens when two Archeologists stumble into a marijuana field?

They make joint discovery!

24. If someone says you're queer, then what are the odds?

25. How is a bartender like a shoe salesman?

First, they help you tie one on, then, give you the boot when you can't stand up!

26. Why did the Native American fuck the Porsche sales lady in the ass?

He wanted to see how she performed with a rear Injun!

27. What do a stripper and a runner have in common?

After three laps, their legs are killing them!

28. Where do most conspiracy nuts end up?

In a cemetery surrounded by plots!

29. Why did the suspect think the cop was gay?

The cop did a full body cavity search, then looked at the suspect and said, "You're next!"

30. Why did the fast-food joint call their new item Spartan French Fires?

Because they were made with ancient grease!

31. How is life like a prostitute?

You could get screwed at every corner.

32. Did you hear about the new bar in Alaska called the Periodic Table?

The only people that go there are the ones willing to go out into the elements.

33. What makes scientist drunk?

Theorem! (The rum)

34. A man went to his doctor and complained

that his feet hurt. The doctor examined him and said, "Stop putting yourself in other people's shoes."

The Doctor asked if there were any other problems. The guy said, "Well, I was going to tell you my dick hurts."

35. What do you call a Native American with four motorcycles?

A four-cycle Injun!

36. Why did Robin Hood's men think he was gay?

Because he kept throwing his meat in the friar!

37. What did Noah use to keep his rivets in place?

An arc welder!

38. Why was the celebrity upset?

The results of her urinalysis were leaked to the press!

39. Why did the investment banker frequent the whore house?

He spent all day making his bucks in bonds, and he spent all night in buxom blonds!

40. Why did the hillbilly find it hard to run across the wheat field?

He was going against the grain!

41. What do coal powered generators have in common with rock bands?

They both rely on ample fires!

42. What could you call a lesbian couple?

Two halves of the same hole!

43. What's the definition of a casket?

A self-storage unit!

44. Did you hear about the contest at the gallows for a noose tying to competition?

Two guys were neck and neck!

45. Did you hear about the prostitute that only had sex with sailors?

Her income was fleeting!

46. Why is it a bad idea to date Playboy models?

They have issues!

47. How is credit like a prostitute?

You have to pay a fee to go in the hole!

48. When Paul asked a girl to fuck him, sometimes he would take a knee to the groin.

One night he took four knees to the groin. Tiffany, Courtney, Whitney, Stephanie!

49. What has the popularity of breast implants done for the bra manufacturers?

They have seen an increase in their material holdings!

50. Did you hear about the new makeup for transvestites?

It's called Lori-AL!

51. Why did the gay lumber jack have so much work?

He was a backlogged!

52. What does Congress have in common with a gay bar?

They are both full of cock suckers and fucking assholes!

53. Why did the guards at the prison like to hang out with the executioners?

They knew all the swingers!

54. Why does UPS like hiring ex-prostitutes?

They are good package handlers!

55. Why wasn't the gay magazine accepting work from freelance writers

They had enough staff to handle the current load!

56. What did the Invisible Man do when he was accused of murder?

He cleared himself!

57. What do flashers and bad drivers have in common?

They both pull out in front of you without warning!

58. How can you tell if someone is an old fart?

They get more distinct!

59. Why don't prostitutes like eunuchs?

They are detested!

60. Why do cannibals slap their women?

Battered women are a delicacy!

61. What do you call someone who is not all bad?

Mid-evil!

62. What do you call a prostitute that lets two men drill her at the same time?

A two-bit whore!

63. What do identity theft and vertigo have in common?

You lose your balance!

64. What do you call it when a Pimp says his girls give the best blow jobs?

World of mouth advertising about lip service!

65. What's another name for a butt crack?

The bottom line!

66. Did you hear about the Iraq war veteran that lost both his arms in a bomb attack?

He learned to masturbate with his feet and now he has a two-foot cock!

67. If cable TV has 500 channels, why do men watch the nudist channels?

Because there was nothing on!

68. What do you call it when you crack an egg and a partially developed chick falls out?

Meaty yoker!

69. What do you call it when two male Senators go out with each other?

A government man date!

70. Did you hear about the gigolo that fucked an 80-year-old woman to death?

It was his first expiration date!

71. Why are dead batteries always free?

No charge!

72. What do you call a fart that's not squishy?

Cut and dried!

73. How do you stop your girlfriend from masturbating?

You wiener off!

74. Why don't you ever see lesbian prostitutes?

Because they are always doing laps at the Y!

75. Why did the college professor only buy top quality marijuana?

He had high standards!

76. Why did the vice cop get a medal after getting a blow job from the prostitute?

For staying firm in the face of the enemy despite stiff opposition!

77. Why was the Judge unable to stop the Irishman from masturbating?

It was out of his hands!

78. What do you call a porn star's testicles?

Load stones!

79. What do you get if you add hops to a five-year-old Scotch?

Hop Scotch!

80. How do you know if your wife really knows you?

No sex, no smoking, no beer, no hanging out with the guys!

81. If you don't belly up to the bar, what will happen?

The bar will go belly-up!

82. Why was the American not afraid of being raped in the German prison?

The Warden said, "There will be no ass gape!

83. Why is exercise before you pass away good for your stomach?

It helps you die gist right!

84. What's another name for a chastity belt?

Meat locker!

85. When the cop arrested the prostitute, he told her anything she said would be held against her. What did she say!

Penis!

86. What happened to the lady when the cops yanked the medical marijuana from her hand?

Her fingers were des-jointed!

87. Why didn't the midget have sex with the prostitute?

He didn't feel up to it!

88. When is Mr. Posey not Mr. Posey?

In the morning when he arose!

89. What do you call a card deck of topless large breasted women?

A stacked deck!

90. What is another name for a jock -strap?

Cup-o-noodles!

91. Why don't lawyers need Viagra?

Most of them are already with a firm!

92. What happened when the genetic scientist spilled his latte into his Petri dish?

He creamed his genes!

93. What do you call a man after his prostate surgery?

An ex-spurt!

94. What do you call a gay midget with a big ego?

A cocky little sucker!

95. What do you do with a video of a condom?

Put it on U-tube!

96. Why did the accountant become a prostitute?

She was easily bored.

97. Why was the detective able to light his cigar with the fingerprint?

It was a match!

98. Where do nudists go shopping?

Strip malls!

99. Where were the large quantities of drugs stashed?

In Kilo-cations!

100. Why did the young woman become a prostitute?

She was hard pressed for money!

101. How much money did the prostitute that only did anal sex make?

A butt-load!

102. Where did the rich old lady get her young handsome husband?

From a male-order catalog!

103. Why don't they give credit cards to crazy people?

Because they are unbalanced!

104. Why do ladies feel men's clotches at the bar?

To see if they are up to date!

105. What kind of tics did Noah take with him?

Ark-tics!

106. Why didn't Dr. Watson have to pay any taxes?

Sherlock Holmes gave him some brilliant deductions!

107. How do you give a Blond mental stimulation?

Fuck her in the head!

108. What was the name of the Scarecrow in the Wizard of Oz?

Mr. Hay-Knee!

109. Why did the lesbian bar only serve beer and wine?

No hard lickers were allowed!

110. What do you call a fat guy that can't tell the truth?

Jumboliya!

111. When I asked the pimp if his girls were ambitious, what did he say?

They are all bitches!

112. What's the one word most often heard from British prostitutes?

Focus!

113. If a prostitute is outgoing, what are her customers?

Incuming!

114. What was it called when the Indians drove off the Whites?

Unsettling!

115. Did you hear about the guy that made a door knob out of a dildo?

Some crazy bitch has been banging on his door all night!

116. What happens to a man that constantly thinks about breasts?

He racks his brains!

117. What do you call a Jewish prostitute that is very clever?

Whore-o-wits!

118. Why do cats have nine lives?

They purr sever!

119. What do you call the different things Bat-Man's cape can do?

Capabilities!

120. What do you call a girl that doesn't shave her pussy?

Mattie!

121. Did you hear about the prostitute that swallowed so much sperm that she got drunk?

It was sperm intoxa-fuckation!

122. What did the bootylisious pipm have?

Great hindsight!

123. What do you call two midget lesbians?

A small pair-a-dykes!

124. Did you hear about the Doctor that was offering discount for breast implants?

In extreme cases he charges a flat rate!

125. How did the plumber feel when he got stuck in the toilet?

Flushed!

126. Why should you never fight a fat guy?

He might whale on you!

127. What do you call fishermen that always claim they catch the biggest fish?

Larz!

128. What do you call it when you have a threesome?

An add-a-body experience!

129. Why did the midget prostitute earn less money than the other prostitutes?

She was low incum!

130. Did you hear about the guy that was so constipated that when he struggled to take a crap, he almost threw up?

He was bound and gagged!

131. Why did the lesbian have a square tongue?

She just took it out of the box!

132. Why do ladies like to have sex with nice guys?

They always finish last!

133. What did the Ax murderer say to the married couple?

I'm splitting you up!

134. Did you hear about the Doctor that only did vasectomies?

He was living off a fixed income!

135. What's the good news as housing continues to plumbet?

At least they'll have plumbing!

136. When the cops asked the hillbilly if he corn-holed the co-ed, what did he say?

"No. I stalked her!"

137. What do you call a neighborhood where everyone smokes crack and bitches all day?

A high-rant district!

138. How do you steer a bull?

   Castrate him!

139. What do you call the cum shot of a porn star?

   Pay load!

140. What do rock & roll chicks really dig?

   Amplefuckation!

141. Why do men never join weight watchers?

   They lose inches instead of pounds!

142. Why did the genius get bad migraines?

   His head was smarting!

143. Why did the man think his wife was an angel?

   She harps at him all day!

144. What's one thing a gay guy will never give you?

The straight poop!

145. Did you hear about the guy in divorce court because he didn't like his wife's breast implants?

He said he found them unflattering!

146. When do the cows come home?

When it's pasture bedtime!

147. Why was disarming the soldiers useless?

Because they were foot soldiers!

148. When do the cows leave home?

When the moo'en goes down!

149. What did the hillbilly prostitute love the most?

Mounting Dew Dads!

150. What do you get if you cross an Indian and a Jew?

Someone that only accepts kosher food stamps!

151. What do you call a prostitute with an angry snatch?

Crabby!

152. What was the pimp's favorite way to discipline hos girls?

He liked to lay into them hard!

153. What do you call a prostitute that's not royalty?

A lay person!

154. How do you tell a prostitute's is a she-male?

If she has small breasts and a large pantyhose!

155. What kind of sword do you use to kill women with?

A broad sword!

156. How is a prostitute like a dish washer?

You want to put in a full load before you turn it on!

157. In divorce court, the Judge asked the young man why he wanted a divorce.

"Your Honor, I caught my wife making love to a sausage."

"Is that the only reason?" asked the Judge.

"No, but that's the wurst part!"

158. What do you call it when a baseball player gets hit in the cotch with a bat?

A sack fly!

159. When is it okay to eat a human?

When it's in your alphabet soup!

160. Why did the man cum like a porn star after he had the word "system" tattooed on his dick?

It was system overload!

161. What do you call the breast of a girl that lets her boyfriend tittyfuck her?

Pud-knockars!

162. Did you hear about the guy that bought a jack rabbit ranch from a lizard?

It was a hare raising experience from the gecko!

163. Did you hear about the Mexicans that got caught cuming across the boarder?

The Texas Rangers made them clean it up!

164. How did the cannibal like his women?

A little on the saucy side!

165. What happened when the cheerleader kicked the football player that was thinking with his little head in the groin?

She racked his brains.

166. Why couldn't the underpaid porn star ejaculate?

What do you expect, he was low in cum!

167. What do you get if you cross a Jew with an Indian?

A guy that only bums money to buy Hebrew Beer!

168. What do you call a bar for Lesbian pilots?

A no fly zone!

169. How are sneezes like breasts?

They are best when they come in pairs!

170. Did you hear about the cheerleader that sat on the blind man's face?

She made a spectacle out of herself!

171. Why did the cute twin accountants become prostitutes?

They had the figures for it!

172. What did the twin cannibals share?

A uterus!

173. What do you get if you cross an Indian with a Jew?

Someone who can do a rain dance for forty days and forty nights!

174. Do you know the difference between Father's Day and the Fourth of July?

One is for Father's Day, the other is Forefather's Day!

175. What do you get if you cross a Jew and an Indian?

A man that if he had an uprising in his pants it would be a reserection!

176. What do jewelers make from the diamonds that Africans smuggle out in their rectums?

High end jewelry!

177. What did the Dominatrix and the Fisherman have in common?

They both had some nice paddling gear!

178. How do you know an attorney has erectile dis-function?

When there is no hard evidence!

179. Why did the pimp like to take his vacation in Las Vegas?

He could play Black Jack while his girls helped other men play slots!

180. What do you call it when a gay guy is found dead with a duck stuck in his ass?

I don't know, but I think fowl play was involved!

181. What happens every time we experience inflation?

Our wallets experience deflation!

182. The old lady asked her doctor for some Viagra to help with her osteoporosis. The doctor told her Viagra would not help with her bone density.

She said, "I give them to my husband and it helps with bone density, believe me!

183. What do you get if you cross an Indian and a Jew?

A lawyer that will Sioux you to death!

184. What do you call a car that you only drive in the fall?

An Autumn-mobile!

185. What do you call a Jewish luxury boat?

Yada Yada!

186. Did you hear about the guy with the constant hard-on?

He was finally able to come to grips with it!

187. What do you call a five-foot asshole?

Hi honey, I'm home!

188. What do you call a six-foot asshole?

How was your day dear?

189. When I pried the cowboys sizzling butt off my stove, he looked all wild eyed.

I was certain it was because he was just deranged!

190. What do you call someone that tells on you for having a toupee?

A rug rat!

191. What can you always count on in life?

Your fingers!

192. When the man fell into the mixer at the commercial bakery, why didn't anybody notice?

He just blended in!

193. After taking powerful pain killers, the man's wife said she was going to sleep like a baby.

Her husband said, "Does that mean you're going to wet the bed?"

194. What's so great about a lap dance?

I used to wonder the same thing, but after a while it rubs off on you!

195. Why didn't the prostitute charge

virgins?

She liked working with new cumers!

196. The old man said, "I'm tired of you walking all over me."

The young man said, "Well, you are my step-dad!"

197. Why weren't meals at the cannibal café cheap?

They cost an arm and a leg!

198. What do you call a criminal that is executed in the electric chair?

Currently dead!

199. What is another name for a funeral procession?

A dead line!

200. What do you call it when a man doesn't have sex with his fiancé for six months, but they talk a lot?

A long speaking engagement!

201. What do you call a thousand-dollar wig of a man?

A high price toupee!

202. Why should you never pay attention to what a ghost says?

It's immaterial!

203. What do bartending and prison sex have in common?

It's either bottoms up or down the hatch!

204. How is college like a penis?

It can be hard, but not all the time!

205. What do you call a woman with six breasts?

Bossy!

206. What is the definition of a busy prostitute on an Indian *reservation?*

One that makes a hundred Bucks a night!

207. When a pimp or a madam runs a bunch of prostitutes it's called a prostitution ring. What is it called when they run a bunch of gigolos?

A cock ring!

208. What do you call a physician that runs a detox unit?

A dry Doc!

209. Why did the ship wreck on the invisible man's island?

Because the coast was clear!

210. In divorce court, the judge said, "Let me get this straight, your wife said you were out carousing at night. Is that correct?

The man responded. "That's not what she said your Honor, what she said was that I keep slipping out!"

211. What do you get if you have a ten-inch penis?

Two five-inch penises!

212. What do you get when ten Black ladies are shaking their booties?

A bun dance!

213. Did you hear about the lonely old maid that bought a rubber man to have sex with?

The whole thing blew up in her face!

214.How can you tell if you're working in a stable economy?

You'll be able to smell the bullshit!

215. Why did one lesbian show her strap-on dildo collection to another lesbian?

To prove she had good manners!

216. Why do gay people smile all the time?

They can't keep a straight face!

217. What do you call a 1000-Amp battery with only 600 Amps in *it?*

A large at medium charge!

218. In Alaska, what do you call a guy that smokes marijuana and then freezes to death?

Stoned cold!

219. What do you call a woman that has sex with a guy that has a twelve-inch penis?

Foot loose!

220. How do you know when two lesbians are fishing?

They use a rubber dingy!

221. Did you hear about the guy that took Viagra and passed *away?*

He had a hard attack while having a stroke!

222. Did you hear about the undertaker that used the hands of the dead people to masturbate with?

His son said he was a dead-beat dad!

223. I used to earn my money selling sperm to the sperm bank.

Then I got married and fucked myself out of a job!

224. What do you call a pediatrician on an Indian reservation?

An expert in small Injun repair!

225. Why was the Cannibal Bar and Grill being investigated?

It was rumored they were serving teenagers!

226. At the Catholic school, why were the Nuns such good teachers?

They made my knuckles smart!

227. What's another name for military basic training?

Private school!

228. What do a designated hitter and a taxi driver have in common?

You can count on them to drive you home!

229. What did the seamstress have in common with the gay guy?

They both hem up the bottom!

230. Did you hear about the flat-chested fourteen-year-old girl that spent a summer in reform school?

She busted out!

231. What caused the girls at the all-girl school to get pregnant?

They came in contact with boys!

232. What is a cannibal's favorite student?

Freshmen!

233. What do you call a woman that cleans your house and has sex with you?

A Ho-maid!

234. What do you call the slowest pig at the pig races?

Pokey Pig!

235. Why did the ladies' husband buy her breast implants?

Chest for fun!

236. Why didn't they let the Alzheimer patient drive?

He just loved to get in his car and go, but nobody liked cleaning it up after he went!

237. What do you call it when a guy flashes a couple women with his two-inch cock?

Knob seen!

238. Did you hear about the prostitute that only did hand jobs?

She was working her fingers to the bone for a five-digit income!

239. How is a crime spree like sex?

After you do it enough you tend to get sloppy!

240. Why did the drug pusher fire one of his dealers?

He just wasn't moving the same speed as the other dealers!

241. What's one thing that you are sure to have if you go to prison?

Lots of friends on the "inside"!

242. How does a pimp keep track of his prostitute's activities?

By checking their black boxes!

243. What do you call a woman that only enjoys having sex in men's bathroom stalls?

Fucked in the head!

244. What happens if the prostitute gives too many blow jobs?

Her head becomes permanently cocked to one side!

245. Did you hear about the new play on Broadway called "Trader"?

It opened to a sold-out crowd!

246. Why is a subscription to "Pedophile Porn" magazine such a good deal?

You get four teen issues for the price of twelve!

247. Did you hear about Pharmacist that told the Porn Actor he could get his condoms

in bulk?

The Porn Actor said, "Great, just my size"!

248. If the scent of a woman is something special, what did the cheap prostitute have?

25 scents!

249. Did you hear about the new Fairy Tail called "Snow White and the 70 Wharfs?

Her favorite Wharf was 69!

250. Did you hear about the thousand dollars a night hooker?

She had a grand opening!

www.ingramcontent.com/pod-product-compliance
Lightning Source LLC
Chambersburg PA
CBHW070943120626
46546CB00004B/1545